The island in this book is a mix of various islands riding in the sea off the coast of the Antarctic Peninsula. Its history is the kind of history these islands could have experienced. Scientists cannot tell exactly what happened to each of the Antarctic islands. Antarctica's remoteness and harsh climate limit scientific investigations. Unpacking the past is especially difficult when ice and snow lie in a thick layer over an island's skin. But important field research is happening in this exciting area, and evidence is accumulating.

Lucia and I travelled along the Antarctic Peninsula with geophysicists and seismologists as they measured plate tectonic movements, learning from them as they battled ashore through freezing seas and scrambled over icy rocks. Later, on an island where fossils lay scattered like shells on a beach, I talked to palaeontologists and palaeobotanists about their discoveries, including five to six-metre-long skeletons of plesiosaurs. There's a picture of one kind of plesiosaur, Kronosaurus, on pages 14-15.

The text has been discussed with US scientists in Antarctica, and with scientists in London and the British Antarctic Survey in Cambridge. We are very grateful to all the scientists who have helped with this project, in particular to the book's consultant, Dr David Cantrill. We are also grateful to the US National Science Foundation Artists & Writers Program for the opportunity to work in Antarctica.

The island in this book does not have a name. But to me – it's Survival Island.

Antarctic Peninsula

South Pole

The Island
that Moved

The Forces that
Shape our Earth

MEREDITH HOOPER

illustrated by **Lucia deLeiris**

FRANCES LINCOLN CHILDREN'S BOOKS

Imagine an island. It's beautiful. Bold. Wild.

Imagine landing on the beach. Whale bones lie above the racing surf.
Planks of wood spill over the grey sand, washed up from a sailing ship
wrecked who knows where, who knows when. It's summer. Fat elephant seals
sleep in steamy heaps, belching and grunting. Chinstrap penguins skitter
past with food for their chicks.

Behind the beach, mountains reach into the clouds. A glacier slowly
shifts its white bulk towards the sea.

No humans live on the island. No humans have ever lived here.

7

No trees or bushes grow on the island. The only plants are tufts of grass,
and mounds of mosses, and lichens clutching the rocks, crusty
deep orange, mould black, frilly silver-grey. Mites and springtails
scuttle through old penguins' nests, and shelter under stones.
They eat algae and fungi, or each other. Only the tiniest animals
can live here all year round.

Because this island is at the bottom of the world.
It rises out of the ice-strewn ocean, frozen,
lonely, magnificent.

But beneath the toes of penguins, the delicate legs of minuscule insects, the island is moving. It moves, all the time, through the wide ocean. The speed a fingernail grows.

The land that became this island was once molten rock,
slowly shifting deep beneath the bed of the ocean,
eight kilometres down inside Earth's crust.

Gradually the molten rock began rising up and spilling
on to the sea-floor. Hissing, seething, heaving out
in red-hot pillowy lumps of lava. Cooled by seawater
to black hard rock. Forming ridges, building higher,
spreading outwards as new sea-floor. Covered by
layers of fine ooze, by the skeletons of minute animals,
and the delicate shells of sea creatures
drifting in death down through the depths.

11

200 million years ago, most of the continents on Earth were gathered into one great supercontinent called Pangaea. The southern part, called Gondwana, included Africa, South America, Australia and India, with Antarctica at the centre. Gondwana was like a huge jigsaw puzzle with all the pieces still in place.

Herds of dinosaurs roamed the great plains and grazed along the shores of muddy lakes. Huge Cryolophosaurs hunted for prey amongst the tree ferns and cycads.

Earth's climate was warm and wet, Earth's surface lush and pulsing with life.

Earth's skin is made of hard, cold rock in separate pieces, like giant plates, floating on top of hot molten rock. The plates butt up against each other, jostling and moving in massive slow motion, pushed and pulled by processes deep below. The plates are like a rind, a crust, on the surface of a full fiery bucket.

150 million years ago, the plates that had come together to make Gondwana were starting to break apart into separate pieces, like a cracking paving stone. Enormous fragments beginning to unhook, split off, move away, centimetre by slow centimetre.

Deep inside the ocean, the land that became the island was being dragged along as part of the sea-floor. Slowly grinding forward until it scraped against the edge of Gondwana. Crunching in, plastering on along the coast of Antarctica, bit by bit. Blocky hunks and ripped-off lumps, rocks from the ocean crust and ancient muds, all left behind high and dry, as the piece of sea-floor they were riding on was forced down under the continent's edge.

Fern spores blowing on the wind lodged in cracks
between the rocks. Flies buzzed and hovered.
Kronosaurs heaved out of the surf to lay their eggs on the
new shore. Cockroaches scuttled through the undergrowth.

100 million years ago, the new land was filled with the scent of plants,
the rustling of insects, the calls of animals.

15

30 million years ago, Australia had unhooked from Gondwana. India and Africa were long gone. South America was finally breaking free. Only Antarctica was left, a lonely continent straddling the South Pole.

Cold deep ocean entirely surrounded Antarctica, isolating it from warmer seas to the north. Wild gales began to howl around the continent. Temperatures started to drop. Dry winds blew with ice in their breath. Glittering white ice-caps spread across Antarctica's mountains. Forests began to die. Shivering animals searched for shelter. Unrelenting cold was stripping the living continent of its rich, varied life.

But on Antarctica's edge, along the coast, saplings still reached towards the low slanting sunlight. Here, in the land that became the island, flowers still bloomed in sheltered valleys and animals could find a safe haven.

Four million years ago, the land that became the island began to separate from the rest of Antarctica. The crust of the continent started stretching, creating a wide rift valley where dwarfed trees, stressed by the cold, could find shelter.

The rift valley stretched further, sagging like a piece of pulled chewing gum. The sea spilt in, salt water drowning the little shrunken forest. Now, the land that became the island was marooned by the spilling sea, split off from the continent it had been joined to.

The rift widened and deepened, widened and deepened. Then fractured. Boiling lava welled up through the fracture from deep within the earth, to harden and cool as new sea-floor.

On the outside edge of the rift, hills and valleys were being pulled
further and further away from their old anchorage.
Broken by the surging sea into a line of islands. At the end of the line,
new-formed shores gnawed at by relentless surf, lay our island.

The island continued slowly drifting, pushed outwards by the spreading
sea-floor. Powerful ocean currents swirled along a trench-like strait,
separating the island from the ever-more-distant mainland of Antarctica.

Three million years ago, ash and debris fell on to the island. Coating the hills, filling the valleys, smothering every growing thing. The ash fell from a thick black sky, catapulted up in roaring scorching columns by distant volcanoes. Fiery orange streams of lava glowed through the gritty, acrid ash-gloom.

Earthquakes shook the island's mountains. Rocks tumbled loose, bumping and crashing. Tidal waves swept inland, destroying, drowning.

Three quarters of a million years ago, nothing crawled or fluttered on the island. Nothing grew on it. Intense, deep cold had crushed all living things. The island was trapped under a heavy load of ice. The ice groaned as it ground over the rocks beneath, gouging out valleys, scraping and reshaping the land. The ice spread over the frozen sea, which had shrunk, and reduced, because so much of Earth's water had now turned into ice. The air was filled with sharp cracking sounds as the ice shifted, with roars and rumbles as it slipped and tumbled. Summer's light, winter's darkness, brought no change.

The island was gripped in an ice age. An ice age lasting tens of thousands of years.

11,000 years ago, the most recent of Earth's ice ages started to ease.
Glaciers retreated, and the sea level rose with water from melting ice.

Salt water now surged higher around the island's edges. But the mountains
still felt the weight of grinding glaciers. Winter blizzards still howled
and battered. Here in the south, the island hunched under winter snow
as Antarctic cold reached out and gripped.

Yet life came back. Moss spores drifted in on the winds. Giant petrels,
scouring the oceans for food, found ledges along the cliffs to raise
their summer chicks. Penguins scrabbled ashore and collected pebbles
to build their nests. Elephant seals hauled up on the beaches,
and the females gave birth to furry pups with glistening eyes.

With its small precious cargo of twenty-first century living things,
our island keeps moving.

Out through the ocean. Two centimetres a year.

25

EARTH'S SKIN

We are all on islands that move. And keep moving.

The theory that great plates move over the surface of the Earth
with continents on their backs is called 'plate tectonics'.
The ideas of plate tectonics help us explain the workings
of our Earth.

Where the plates that make up Earth's skin meet,
huge pressures, stresses and strains can build up.

Sometimes plates slide
and grate past each
other in short abrupt
slips, and sudden
jerks, resulting
in earthquakes.

Sometimes the edge of one plate
rides over the edge of another plate.
The part underneath sinks down
and melts in the great heat of the hot,
molten rock beneath the plates,
the Earth's mantle. Most volcanoes
are located on plate boundaries.

New crust forms where the plates
are pulled apart. Molten lava wells up
from deep inside the Earth and hardens,
creating new plate material to fill the
gap, pushing the plates further apart.

Sometimes two plates collide. The impact
can squeeze and crumple the rocks between
them to form mountains, accompanied
by earthquakes and volcanic eruptions.

Mount Everest in the Himalayas is made of rock that was once deep under the sea.
The disintegrating shells of sea creatures lie on its summit. India collided with Asia
50 million years ago. Since then it has travelled 2000 kilometres further north.
The continuing collision pushes the Himalayan mountains up ever higher, one to three
centimetres a year. But glaciers, rivers and heavy rain keep eroding them down again.

Events that can drive a slab of marine rock thousands of feet into the air have
happened on Earth before. They will happen again. Earth's surface is in constant,
slow-motion turmoil. Nothing today looks the way it once looked, or the way
it used to look before that.

GONDWANA BREAKS APART

Look at the shapes of the continents on our Earth.
The bump of South America tucks into the hollow
of Africa. The curve of Australia mirrors
the curve of Antarctica directly below.
It's possible to see how the coastlines
match and how the continents
fitted together, before
they came apart.

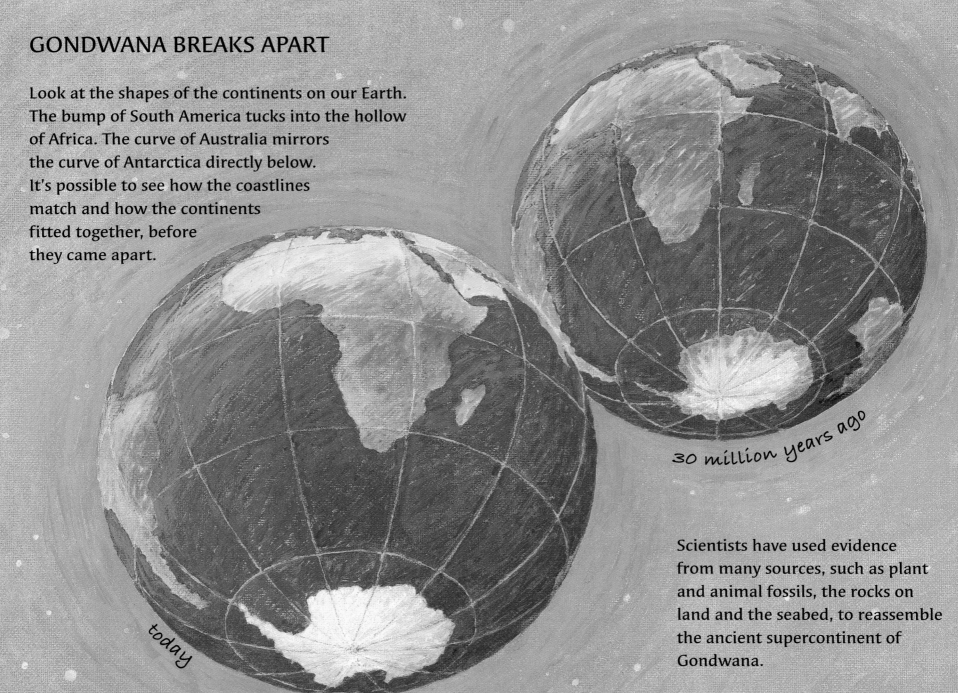

30 million years ago

today

Scientists have used evidence
from many sources, such as plant
and animal fossils, the rocks on
land and the seabed, to reassemble
the ancient supercontinent of
Gondwana.

28

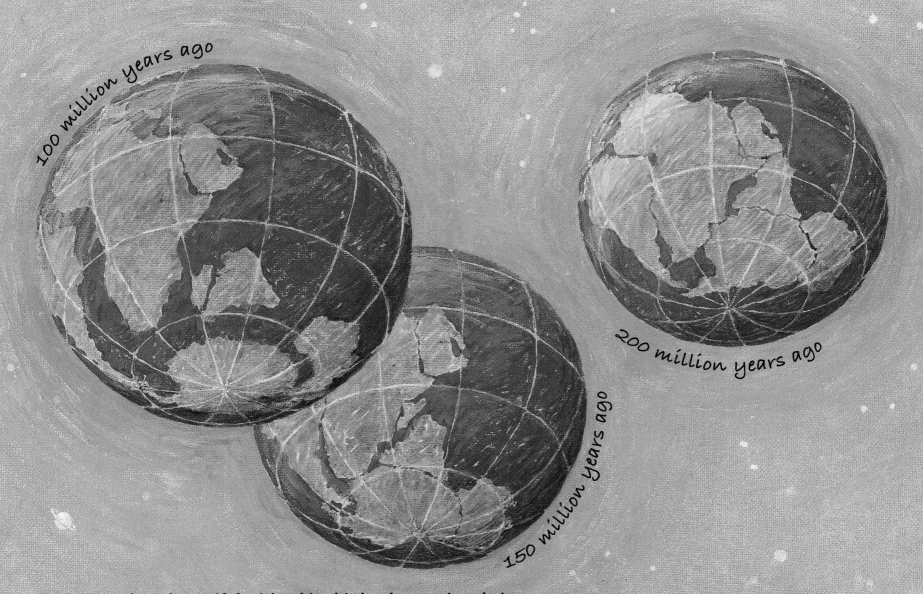

100 million years ago

200 million years ago

150 million years ago

Scientists don't know if the island in this book came into being exactly the way it has been described. Some of the animals illustrated are the kinds we would expect, but we don't know exactly what they would have looked like. New discoveries are being made all the time. There are still many questions that need answers.

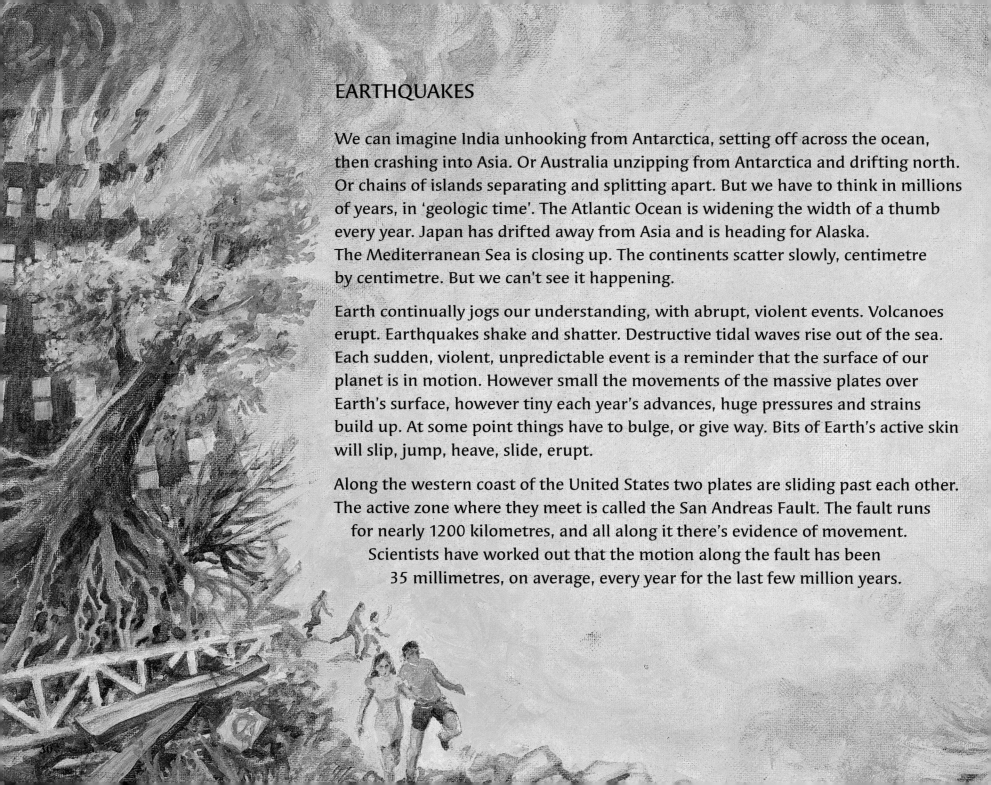

EARTHQUAKES

We can imagine India unhooking from Antarctica, setting off across the ocean, then crashing into Asia. Or Australia unzipping from Antarctica and drifting north. Or chains of islands separating and splitting apart. But we have to think in millions of years, in 'geologic time'. The Atlantic Ocean is widening the width of a thumb every year. Japan has drifted away from Asia and is heading for Alaska. The Mediterranean Sea is closing up. The continents scatter slowly, centimetre by centimetre. But we can't see it happening.

Earth continually jogs our understanding, with abrupt, violent events. Volcanoes erupt. Earthquakes shake and shatter. Destructive tidal waves rise out of the sea. Each sudden, violent, unpredictable event is a reminder that the surface of our planet is in motion. However small the movements of the massive plates over Earth's surface, however tiny each year's advances, huge pressures and strains build up. At some point things have to bulge, or give way. Bits of Earth's active skin will slip, jump, heave, slide, erupt.

Along the western coast of the United States two plates are sliding past each other. The active zone where they meet is called the San Andreas Fault. The fault runs for nearly 1200 kilometres, and all along it there's evidence of movement. Scientists have worked out that the motion along the fault has been 35 millimetres, on average, every year for the last few million years.

But this does not happen in a regular tiny creep. The strains of the Pacific plate tugging north-west past the North American plate are released in sudden, brief, violent, destructive moments. A mountain range can shift six metres north-west in a couple of seconds. The land beneath a road can rise a metre, as if it's been suddenly punched up from below. The side of a mountain can explode away. Houses shake, and collapse.

In an earthquake the two great slanting faces of the plates might suddenly shift against each other, nine kilometres down under the ground. But the shocks are felt up on the surface for hundreds of kilometres in each direction. Proof of the forces that are changing the face of our planet, all the time.

Proof that our islands are moving.

TIME LINE FOR THE ISLAND

Geologists divide the Earth's history into various time periods, from its beginnings, around 4600 million years ago (mya), to the present.

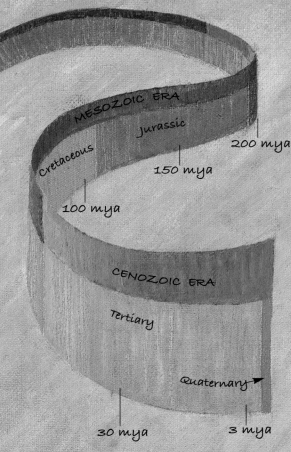

MESOZOIC ERA

Cretaceous

Jurassic

200 mya

150 mya

100 mya

CENOZOIC ERA

Tertiary

Quaternary

30 mya

3 mya

INSIDE THE EARTH

EARTH'S CRUST is a thin, cold, solid layer, made up of separate rocky plates which butt up against each other. The crust is about seven kilometres thick under the ocean and about 35 kilometres thick under continents. The biggest plates are rigid. Small plates can be squeezed, or bent.

The LITHOSPHERE is made up of the crust and the upper few kilometres of the mantle.

The MANTLE is a hot, solid, rocky layer that can move, rather like solid ice moves in a glacier. The mantle is 2900 kilometres thick and surrounds the core.

Beneath the mantle is a CORE of molten iron. The temperature at the outside edge of the core is about 4000 degrees C. The very centre of the core is solid iron rock. The temperature here is probably 6000 degrees C.

32

For Fred – M.H.
For Alain and Mary – L. deL.

The Publishers would like to thank Dr David Cantrill
from the Swedish Museum of Natural History
for checking the text and illustrations.

First published in Great Britain in 2004 by
Frances Lincoln Children's Books, 4 Torriano Mews,
Torriano Avenue, London NW5 2RZ

www.franceslincoln.com

British Library Cataloguing in Publication Data
available on request

ISBN 1-84507-003-8

Printed in Singapore

10 9 8 7 6 5 4 3 2 1